Made in the USA
Monee, IL
20 March 2022

93229756R00057